Happy
Birthday,
( )

"books for kids"

KIWANIS INTERNATIONAL

K

success through reading

A Detroit *www.kiwanis1.org* Service Project

D0907683

When I was a little boy, I wanted to be an historian more than anything in the world. My mother, who was a very encouraging person, suggested I write a short history about each of the places we visited on vacation for practice.

My little sister, Katie, got wind of this project. She had her own ideas. She collected stuffed animals, Jody the mouse, being her favorite. She was convinced that this bedraggled rodent had been sold to her by a wise man, who had given it the power of speech. She wanted to be sure I made a record of Jody's life and teachings. Of course, I didn't want to do any such thing. Katie sulked and cried until our mother said it would be good for me to learn how to work with "source materials," by which she meant my sister's wild claims about her dumb toy. I finally threw up my hands and dedicated my talents to remembering my sister's misadventures with Jody. Whenever possible, I also incorporated the history of the place we were visiting. The result of all of this is that, in my old age, I have become an historical novelist, which only goes to show that parents have a great deal to do with what their children eventually become in life.

Great Places
Jody's Michigan Adventures
Michigan's Greenfield Village

Summary: Kevin's 9-year-old cousin, Elliot, is staying with
the Murphys for the summer. Elliot loves science. On
Kevin's advice, Elliot decides to visit the Henry Ford
Museum so he can learn how the Quadricycle is made.
Kevin's little sister, Katie, and her best friend, Jihan, go to
Greenfield Village while the boys are at the museum.

Written by Leigh A. Arrathoon & John Davio
Illustrated by Kenneth M. Hajdyla
Coloring by Mary Anne Strong

If you want more information on
Paint Creek Press publications
visit: www.paintcreekpress.com
or write for a free brochure.
Paint Creek Press, Ltd.
620 Miller Ave.
Rochester, MI 48307

ISBN 1-893047-00-8

Katie Murphy

Kevin Murphy

Elliot

Jihan

Jody

Vernabelle

Last summer was hot and crazy. The crazy part was my nine-year-old cousin, Elliot. He was visiting us for a whole two months. My name is Kevin Murphy, by the way.

Elliot wants to be a scientist. He took apart watches like Henry Ford used to do. After he ruined Katie's cat clock, and my best wrist watch, he decided it might be better to build **gliders** (planes without motors), like the Wright brothers did. He had seen the Wright aircraft at the Smithsonian Institute in Washington D.C., where he lives.

One afternoon, my little sister Katie and I were playing checkers on the back porch. Jody, Katie's stuffed Dutch mouse from Holland, Michigan, and her new toy friend, named Vernabelle, were giving her advice. Vernabelle is a sheep. Katie got her from our aunt Elizabeth. Our aunt lives in Bilbury - a town in a part of England known as the Cotswolds.

I jumped a lot of checkers. Katie was very angry. Jody and Vernabelle tried to give her advice. They wanted her to win.

All of a sudden, a cry rang out from the maple tree.

"Hey Kev! Look at me!"

We all looked. There was Elliot, perched in the treetop with his home-made **biplane** (an airplane with two sets of wings - one above the other).

"How did you get that thing all the way up there? I yelled.

It was too late for conversation. The glider had already launched. It dropped like a stone and collapsed under the tree.

Elliot was nowhere in sight. Katie and I ran to the glider. Vernabelle covered her eyes with her hooves.

I pulled back the cloth from over the **cockpit** (the place where the pilot sits). I guess I expected to find Elliot inside. No one.

"Maybe he was thrown clear," Katie suggested.

"Nope," I said. I had seen him.

"He's in the tree," I said.

Elliot jumped lightly to the ground from the lowest branch. Then he stuffed his hands in his pants pockets.

"Too much **drag**,"* he sighed.

"You mean, no **lift**** at all!" I sneered.

"We thought you were dead!" said Katie.

"Oh," Elliot shrugged. "You thought I was in the plane? No. The Wright brothers flew their first glider as a kite. So did I."

Katie stared hard at Elliot. "Why are you in that stupid get-up?" she said at last.

"Oh, you mean the suit?" Elliot asked, straightening his tie. "The Wrights always dressed up, no matter what."

"You're nuts!" Katie said. "I liked it better when you thought you were young Henry Ford. Then you just took apart all our watches."

*One of several things that can slow the plane down. Basically, anything that gets in the way of the airflow 'drags' on the plane.
**Lift is the upward pressure of slow-moving air beneath the wing that opposes the downward pull of gravity. Gravity is the constant downward pull of the earth's center. Because of gravity, the plane's weight works against the lift of the air pressure.

"Hmm," said Elliot, ignoring Katie. He didn't do this to hurt her feelings. He was thinking about something important. He pulled on his eyebrow - this was what he always did when he was thinking. Finally, he spoke.

"I ought to build a car like Henry's 1896 **Quadricycle.*** What do you think Kev?"

"Well, I don't know if we could do it, but it's a whole lot safer than jumping out of trees in a glider," I answered.

"I think you're both crazy," said Katie. "How're you guys going to know what goes into a thing like the Quadricycle? I mean, it must have a zillion parts."

"I know. We'll go to the Henry Ford Museum and Greenfield Village," I offered. "It's in Dearborn. We can just copy the Quadricycle they've got there."

"Yeah!" said Elliot.

"I get to invite my girlfriend, Jihan," Katie said. After all, it's pretty boring for a girl to have to spend time with two boys and a dumb car."

*Henry Ford's first car had a gasoline compression engine, but it was made largely of bicycle parts.

Nobody had thought about Katie. If she brought Jihan, it could be a real pain to worry about two little girls. I had an idea.

"You and Jihan can go to Greenfield Village," I told her. "It's right next door to the Henry Ford Museum. That way you and Jihan can explore the houses the inventors lived in and the shops where they worked. We'll meet you when we're through looking at the cars, planes, locomotives, and steam engines those men created. Okay?"

Katie was delighted. She didn't want to see any planes or cars.

"Vernabelle," she said, "We can see the wonderful Cotswold Cottage. It's in Greenfield Village. It'll be like visiting Aunt Elizabeth at Bibury. You'll love it!"

Vernabelle started to cry. She was homesick. Katie took her in the house for tea and cakes.

When we told my parents about our plan, my father was against it at first. How would we get to Dearborn alone? Finally, my mother decided to take us. She could go to the Village with the girls.

When the day came for our visit to The Henry Ford Museum and Greenfield Village, the sky was bright blue. The weather was perfect. We all piled into my mother's station wagon.

When we got to the museum, we saw big brick buildings, with white trim. The Henry Ford Museum Entrance was the grandest building I'd ever seen. It was a copy of Independence Hall in Philadelphia.

We guys went straight to the Henry Ford Museum. The trains were the first thing we saw. Neither of us said so, but we both wanted to go to the Grand Trunk Depot, where Thomas Edison had been a newsboy. Unfortunately, the museum doesn't have that train. But they do have one that is made from the parts of several trains from the same time as the Grand Trunk.

Thomas Edison worked as a "news butch," which means he sold newspapers, fruit, and candy to people on the train. He was only twelve years old at the time.

Thomas Edison was born in Milan, Ohio on February 11, 1847. They called him "Al" because his middle name was "Alva."

Milan was a busy canal town. It had a tannery, a blacksmith, a lumberyard, and Al's father's shingle mill. When the railroad was built, it passed by Milan. Barges were no longer needed to carry goods. This meant that the town died. The Edisons had to move to Port Huron, Michigan.

Al was a sickly little boy. He never went to school until he was $8^{1/2}$ years old. Then his teacher, the Reverend B. Engel, was so mean, that he only stayed in the school for six months. Al could never do well because he asked too many questions.

One day Al overheard his teacher say that he was "**addled**" (confused). He ran home crying. His mother went to school to tell the Reverend Engel off. She had been a school teacher too. She knew her son was gifted. Edison used to say that his mother was the making of him. She made him feel that he had someone to live for, someone he must not disappoint.

Elliot is a lot like Thomas Edison - a nice boy, really bright, but always in trouble. He's always experimenting, asking questions, and wrecking things.

When he was really little, Al sat on Lulu the goose's eggs because he thought he could hatch them faster than she could. He broke all the eggs.

Next he set fire to his father's barn because he wanted to see what fire "did." His father was very angry!

One time Al talked his friend, Michael Otis, into swallowing some **Seidlitz powder** (a bubbling laxative). Michael was supposed to fly. Instead, he got sick to his stomach. Al's mother put a lock on his chemical laboratory in the basement.

When he was seven, Al had scarlet fever. This damaged his hearing. Then when he was working for the railroad, he became deaf.

It was the time of the Civil War - the battle of Shiloh. Al had figured out that by telegraphing the headlines to the stations before the train arrived, he could get people to buy more papers.

When Al was working for the railroad, he heard about the Battle of Shiloh over the telegraph wires. He bought extra papers. He sold many of them at a much higher price than usual because news about the battle was so much in demand. He was selling newspapers when the train started to pull out without him.

He ran after the train, his arms full of papers. The conductor pulled him up onto the moving car by the ears. According to legend, Al couldn't hear much anymore.*

There are many stories about Thomas Edison's boyhood. What is important is that, when he grew up, he invented many wonderful things: the phonograph, the telephone, the telegraph, moving pictures, xrays, the stock ticker, the battery, and the electric car.

We don't use all of the things Thomas Edison worked on, but he discovered early versions of things we do use. He had 1,093 patents - more than any other inventor in history. He was a poor boy who helped people all over the world.

*The truth is that he had already lost a good deal of his hearing when he had rheumatic fever.

Henry Ford met Thomas Edison on a trip to New York in 1896. Henry wanted to build a gasoline engine. Even though Edison was working on the electric car, he recognized the worth of Henry's idea. He encouraged him. The **Quadricycle** (four-wheeled vehicle) was the result of Henry's hard work and Edison's praise.

Henry and Al became best friends. Henry said Edison was the world's greatest inventor and its worst businessman. Ford built the Edison Institute (now called The Henry Ford, home to the Henry Ford Museum and Greenfield Village) to honor Edison's achievements.

Even though Elliot and I didn't go to Greenfield Village, my sister, Katie, told me about her visit in excrutiating detail.

The lady at the front desk gave my sister and her friend, Jihan, a map. Jihan said she really wanted to visit Luther Burbank's birthplace, as well as Washington Carver's first home. She knew the Hermitage Slave Houses were near there too, and she wanted to see them. She said her great, great grandparents had lived in houses like these.

I guess Vernabelle started to whine.

"You promised to take me to the Cotswolds," she bleated.

"Yes," said Katie, "We're going to see the Ackley Covered Bridge, the Cape Cod Windmill, the Cotswold Cottage and Forge, Noah Webster's House, and the Stephen Foster Memorial."*

"Well, I want to ride on the Suwanee Steamboat," Jody said. "And I'm thirsty too."

"All right," Katie smiled patiently - She smiled just like our mother.

"I'll carry him," Jihan offered. Jody liked Jihan because she was very gentle. She sang to him too.

On the way to Burbank's office, they passed the house where Henry Ford was born - in Dearborn, Michigan. Nearby, was his shop on Bagley Avenue in Detroit. That's where he made the Quadricycle. When the car was all finished, it was too big to roll out the door, so Henry had to chop down part of the wall.

*According to Christian Overland, The Henry Ford Museum & Greenfield Village, recent research proves that the building at Greenfield Village is not Stephen Foster's house.

Next they passed by the Wright Brothers' home and Cycle Shop. It was a simple place. You can hardly believe the airplane was invented there. The brothers built the planes. They tested different kinds of wings and propellers right in the bicycle shop.

After that came Thomas Edison's laboratory from Menlo Park. It is full of chemicals, but it is clean. Edison said that Henry Ford had copied it almost perfectly - except that, in real life, he, and the men who worked with him, were never so neat!

The girls turned right, past the Sarah Jordan Boardinghouse. This is the place where Edison's New Jersey scientists used to live. It was the first house to have electric lights. The girls also passed the laboratory Edison had in Fort Myers, Florida. Finally, they arrived at the Burbank Garden Office. Jihan recognized it right away.

"There's the little office that used to be in Burbank's experimental gardens at Santa Rosa, California!" Jihan exclaimed.

"How do you know?" Katie asked her.

"Well, it says right here on the map."

In the same group of buildings, they saw the place where Burbank was born - in Lancaster, Massachussets - and his store. Jihan knew a lot about him.

"Luther Burbank was born March 7, 1849. He didn't go to Santa Rosa until 1875. But he dreamed about California since he was a small boy," Jihan said.

"When Luther was a little boy, he found a beautiful daisy. He tore off his shirt-tail to tie around the plant so that he could find it again. His mother was pretty mad at him for ruining his shirt. But he never changed. He marked plants with pieces of his ties or shirts all his life.

"While he was still in Massachussetts, Luther was lucky to find a seed ball in one of his potato plants. Usually farms cut potatoes up. The parts that had **eyes** (buds) were planted. Naturally the plants that came from these potato eyes were identical to their parents. But Luther knew the seeds he had found could produce a different kind of potato. The wind or a bee might have carried them from unknown parents.

"When Luther planted the seeds, a new potato was created. The old potatoes were small and red. Some of the new ones were pure white with brown skins. They were called the 'Burbank Potato'.

"When he finally moved to California, Burbank was able to do marvellous things. He proved that man can direct nature. Whereas nature takes thousands of years to change, man can change nature in a very short time.

"Burbank was called the 'Wizard of Horticulture'. He was also known as the 'Edison of Horticultural Mysteries'. Some of his best-known 'creations' are the Satsuma plum, the Crimson California Poppy, the Rosy-Colored Pear, and the Shasta Daisy. He also created a white blackberry, a **plumcot** (a plum mixed with an apricot), and the first double gladioli, to name a few.

"Finally, Luther Burbank produced a dwarf apple tree with different kinds of apples on it. This tree was for his little brother, Alfie, who hurt himself while trying to pick apples from a big tree."

"Jihan," Katie said, "How did you learn so much about Luther Burbank?"

"I did a book report on him," Jihan replied.

They made their way back down to the Ackley Covered Bridge.

Katie knew that the Ackley Covered Bridge was originally built in the 1830s in southwestern Pennsylvania. Henry Ford had the bridge taken apart. Then he had the pieces brought to Michigan. Here the bridge was put back together again as good as new. It was placed beside a beautiful pond with lots of ducks and great big shade trees - just across from Luther Burbank's Garden Office and Store.

"Most of the buildings in this village got here the same way as the bridge," Katie told Jihan. "They were purchased and transported to the village, where they were rebuilt to look like new."

"How do you know that?" asked Jihan.

"My mom got a book on Greenfield Village," Katie answered, winking at Mrs. Murphy.

Once they crossed the Ackley Bridge, Jihan got out her map.

"Let's see. Where are we going? Do you want to see Susquehana Plantation or Plympton House?"

"No. Not now anyway. I want to see the Cape Cod Windmill. Then let's go to the Cotswold Cottage," said Katie. "Vernabelle will be so disappointed if we don't spend some time there."

Vernabelle's ears perked up. She was anxious to see a place that reminded her of home.

"Who lived there?" Jihan asked Katie.

"I don't know, but I sure love the Cotswolds. It's a place in England. I've seen pictures. There are beautiful limestone houses with walled gardens and lazy streams. I want to visit Bibury. My Aunt Elizabeth lives there."

"Me too!" yelled Vernabelle, "When are we going?" She was very sad when no one payed any attention to her.

"Well here we are at the windmill," said Jihan. "This is a seventeenth-century Cape Cod Windmill from West Yarmouth, Massachusetts. The sails have to be spread with canvas so they can catch the wind. As the blades turn, so does the roof. This is how our ancestors ground their grain."

"Wow," Katie said. "Pretty smart!"

"Pretty slow!" said Jihan.

They walked on past the Daggett Farmhouse to the Cotswold **Forge** (place where iron and metal are worked by hammer and heat).

This forge looked just like an old barn on the outside. It is the oldest working blacksmithery in the United States. The village craftsmen make wrought iron household utensils and farm tools there. It was built about 1620 at Snowshill in southwestern England.

Between the forge and the Cotswold Cottage was a stone dovecote - a place where doves live. It's shaped like a cone, with a pointed slate roof and a weather vane on top. The people who lived there ate the doves.

Very near the dovecote was the beautiful seventeenth-century limestone Cotswold Cottage. It had a walled garden. The gate was wooden; the walls were made of stone like the house. Vernabelle's eyes filled with tears.

If Vernabelle thought the outside of the cottage was beautiful, the inside made her weep.

All the furniture was oak. but had been blackened by the fire from the roaring fireplace. Henry Ford had the whole cottage imported from Chedworth, Gloucestershire, also in southwestern England. The Rose Cottage, as it's called, had ivy covered stone walls, a slate roof, and windows with many panes.

Vernabelle didn't want to leave. She tried to hide in a dark corner.

"Come on!" Jody the mouse called. "You'll get left behind."

"I don't care. I like it here."

"Come on you two!" Katie cried. Jihan scooped up Jody, and Katie grabbed Vernabelle.

"No!" Vernabelle shouted, but it was no use.

They left the cottage behind and went on to Noah Webter's house. It had been moved from New Haven, Connecticut to the Village in 1936. It was a grand white frame building, with shuttered windows, and a rounded window in front.

"Boy is that elegant looking!" said Jihan.

"Noah was an elegant guy. He went to Yale you know," Katie said. She knew all about Noah Webster.

"His father, Master Webster, was stern, but patient and loving. He put up with a lot when Noah was going to Yale, because the boy was all puffed up with his own importance.

"Noah's father had to borrow money from his farm to pay for his son's college. At Yale, Noah took Latin, Greek, Theology, and Mathematics. It was during the time of the American Revolution. General George Washington and General Charles Lee came to Yale to visit.

"Noah's father wanted him to learn about agriculture, but Noah didn't want to be a farmer. He liked philosophy and politics.

"He wanted to be a lawyer, but that would cost a lot of money. Noah prayed for direction. He wanted a life that would bring joy to God, honor to his family, and purpose to himself. He decided to teach in order to pay for his studies in law. In 1771, Noah passed his **bar** (law) exam, but there was little work for a lawyer.

"He thought education should be up to the government. School is where children would learn to be patriots. Education would be the heart of the country's strength.

"In 1783, he published the 'Blue-Backed Speller', the first American spelling book. The words to be learned alternated with short readings about truth and values. The books were used for over 100 years. Thirty-five million copies had been sold by 1890.

"Noah became friends with Benjamin Franklin and George Washington before the constitution was drawn up. Although Noah did not get to take part in the constitutional convention, a pamphlet of his, *Sketches of American Policy*, was discussed among the delegates. Many of Noah's ideas appeared in the final draft of the constitution.

"In 1778, Noah married Rebecca (Becca) Greenleaf. Around 1800, Becca suggested to her husband that he write a dictionary. The first version, containing 37,000 words, came out in 1806. In 1807, a 30,000-word version was reproduced for schools.

"In 1811, the family moved to Amherst, where Noah became involved with the new school (1814). He served as its president after it became a college in 1821.

"At age 65, he went to Europe so he could complete his dictionary work. He had to study foreign words, since English comes from European languages. The dictionary was finished in 1828. He invested more money in his publications than he ever took out. His family profited later on.

"Noah Webster died in 1842. Through his books, young people learned language, manners, and patriotism. He said himself that 'What a man does with his life may or may not be remembered after he is gone. . . What matters is that a man's actions are worthy in the eyes of God and useful to his fellow men'."

The Hermitage Slave Houses were sad to look at. Jihan was angry when she saw how poorly her great great grandparents had lived. Katie didn't know what to say. Jody told Jihan,

"Be thankful that now you can go anywhere you want and be everything you can be. If you stay angry at what happened to your ancestors, your anger will keep you from living the beautiful life, just waiting for you and your children."

Jihan's face broke into a soft smile. She loved Jody very much.

The McGuffey Reader was used at the Scotch Settlement School, where Henry Ford was educated. Henry admired the moral teachings of the reader. That's why the McGuffey Schoolhouse is at Greenfield Village. After visiting it, Jihan wanted to see the George Washington Carver Memorial.

"It's my heritage," she said. "George Carver always believed that race problems would be solved by love, that black and white people could just be best friends, like you and me. He was a great man. I want to see where he lived and worked."

"Carver's birthplace was a simple log cabin," Jihan told Katie. "He was born in Diamond Grove, Missouri. His parents were both slaves, but his mother, Mary, belonged to Moses and Susan Carver.

"The Carvers were kindly and didn't really believe in slavery. The boy was known as "Carver's George," until after the Civil War. Then he went to a black school and was called George Carver.

"George loved plants. When he was little, he knew how to make roses grow. Later, in 1890, he went to Simpson Collge in Iowa, where he learned to be an artist. He painted plants.

"George's art teacher, Etta Budd, knew he couldn't make a living as an artist. She encouraged him to go to the Iowa State College of Agriculture and Mechanical Arts, in Ames, Iowa.

"George Carver earned his bachelor of Agriculture degree in 1894. He became a member of the faculty. In 1896, he received his Masters in Agriculture. That year, Carver went to Tuskegee Normal School, in Mecon County, Alabama. That School was run by the famous Booker T. Washington.

"He lived in that place for 47 years. He was the Director of Agriculture there.

"George Carver's greatest contribution was to help black people learn about their soil. He taught them to plant crops that produced nitrogen. The cotton they had always planted wore out the soil by using up all the minerals.

"As part of his effort to help his own people, George developed over 100 products from sweet potatoes and over 300 products from peanuts.

"The outrageously unfair Jim Crow laws forced black people to ride in separate cars of trains. The same laws shamed Carver even when he had to give a speech to white people. If the meeting place was in a hotel, Carver had to come up in the freight elevator!

"When he was 14 years old, Carver witnessed a horrible mob-murder of a black man. That was in Fort Scott, Kansas (March 29, 1879). But he believed that God would settle the race question. In the meanwhile, black people needed to educate themselves to show how valuable they really were.

"George Carver received many honors in his lifetime. Simpson University gave him an honorary doctorate of Science. Henry Ford was among his many powerful friends."

Suddenly it seemed impossible to hold Jody back. He wanted to ride the Suwanee steamboat. He grabbed Vernabelle and raced toward the boat. There, he sang Stephen Foster songs and made a lot of noise.

On the way back from the steamboat, the girls stopped at the Martha Mary Chapel, the Eagle Tavern, and J.R. Jones' General Store. They met us at the Village Entrance Building at 3 P.M.

"But we never got to see the sawmill, the cider mill, the pottery and textile shops, the glass shop, the print shop, the carriage shop, or the carding mill," Katie complained.

"Well, did you at least see the Smith's Creek Station?" I asked. "That's where Edison saved the station master's son." The girls looked blank. "You see," I said, "you missed all the good stuff."

"I'm sure glad you weren't with us," said Jihan. "We had a really good time."

When we got home, Elliot slipped away to think about what he had seen.

Two weeks later we were playing old maid (Katie and Jihan's choice!) on the back porch. Jihan was winning. All of a sudden there was a terrible crash. We looked up, and there was Elliot.

He was sitting at the wheel of what looked exactly like the Quadricycle he and I had seen in the museum. Its front was all crumpled up, where it had collided head-on with the fence.

"Oh oh!" said Elliot. "The steering isn't right."

We all sighed. Elliot is home now, in Washington, D.C. Vernabelle has gotten used to our house, but she still bleats when she thinks of the Rose Cottage at Greenfield Village.